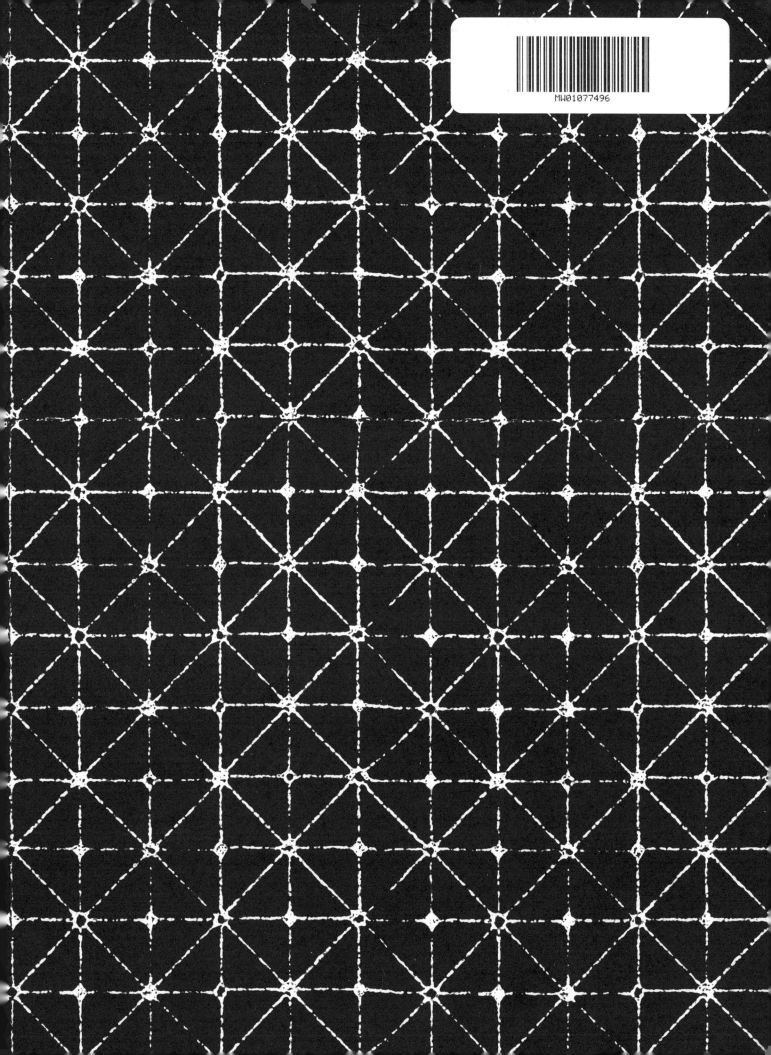

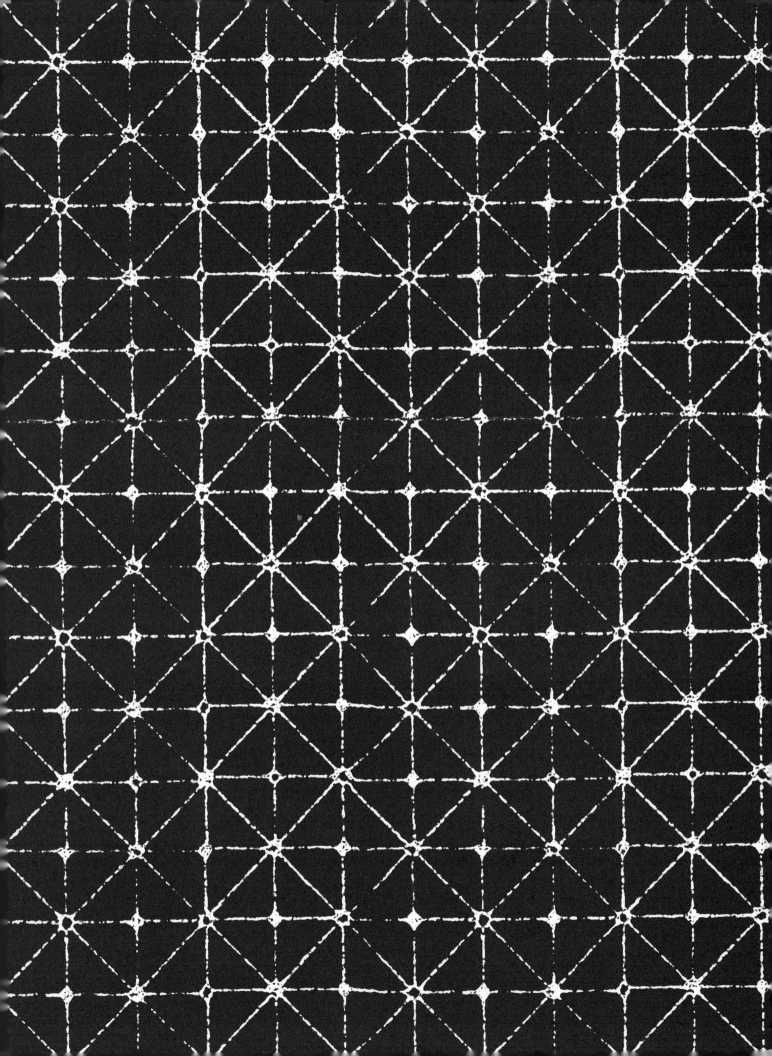

OUTSIDE IN

OUTSIDE IN

INTERIORS BORN FROM NATURE

BRIAN PAQUETTE

Gibbs Smith

CONTENTS

FOREWORD

Amy Kehoe

After first speaking with Brian about this monograph, I followed up our call with a search for photos of where he and his husband spend their weekends in Oregon. I landed on a travel website featuring the Oregon Coast, and an arrestingly simple quote struck me: "There is Magic Here." Paired with imagery of the Haystack Rocks and the surrounding hills, I could easily feel the tremendous beauty of this place. This quote summarized what I interpret Brian's intent is in sharing his second book.

Drawn to the water and its profound influence, Brian is passionately open to the pull of nature. The twists and turns that the natural world thrusts upon us and how we learn to embrace change are guiding principles in his life. He is willing to listen to cues that the natural environment is signaling and interprets them in his work.

Creating environments for clients, designers are tasked with a responsibility to realize individualized spaces that each client can call their own. While there are endlessly beautiful sources of inspiration in the world, it is how Brian approaches designing homes that so deeply ties the process to the groundedness of the natural world. How we feel in our homes matters. What I heard from Brian resonated with me. After a decade in design, there is a desire to pull more deeply from the source in his creative process, a process that counters the endless options that we interface with daily and react with a purposeful slowing down in any given moment.

For interior designers, there is being in nature and all its benefits for our souls and then there is being inspired by nature in the work. The reset of being in the elements, whether walking along the ocean or in the mountains or simply sitting on a park bench, provides us with the opportunity for perspective. Just like taking a few deep breaths can shift a stressful moment, listening to the wind or feeling the sunshine on our face connects us to our larger universe. Finding these connections in our daily lives is refueling and helps with the demand for thousands of small and large decisions on any given project. The "tasking" we all struggle to manage in our lives can be all-consuming. With the seemingly endless tug of to-dos, the importance of interweaving our busy days with a focus on the natural beauty around us is essential to refilling the creative well.

Drawing upon his connection and prioritization of being in nature himself, Brian's interiors are deeply rooted, thoughtful environments. Of particular note is that natural light plays a key role in his projects. His use of sheers and how light is diffused feels like Brian's "magic." His often-tonal spaces stretch the eye and create more expanse in his rooms, like the open sky along the ocean that inspires him. Brian's work is serene, deep, and reliably balanced.

I like to imagine that living in a home designed by Brian I would feel that he has considered the necessity of creating calm. A calm that is enveloping. With that omnipresent force, the senses can start to override the fuss and the noise we are up against every day, and our bodies can restore. And I would think to myself, there is magic here.

INTROSPECTION

Here we are again. It's been a minute. We've all gone through some stuff, huh? Some of us have moved, changed jobs, had kids, got new pets, wore way too much athleisure, and maybe even tried our hands at bread baking. Since the last book, At Home, we have all rediscovered what home means to us and our families. While some of our needs have changed, a few key things have remained the same. We want to create a safe, comfortable, functional, and supportive environment for ourselves and our families. This comes in all shapes and sizes and everyone's needs are different.

I like to think of this book as just the next chapter in my journey as a creative. The last "chapter," or my first book, laid the groundwork, gave some of my personal and creative background, and explored a selection of projects I had completed over a five-year time frame in different locales, with different architecture, and for different people. At our core, we are still a client-driven design firm creating homes for clients. We value quality, comfort, function—"the mix"—and infusing our projects with a host of talented and creative makers and artists. We are constantly evolving and growing, as this is the practice of design. The work throughout this book represents a portion of the past three or so years. Some are ground-up homes that we worked on from the iteration, some are remodels of existing spaces in various scales, and some are furnishings of existing homes for clients who are either new to the spaces or starting fresh chapters with a home they have come to know and love.

Nature and the world around me still play a very big part of what inspires and informs the work. To me, it's at once the easiest and most challenging thing to be inspired by and to dissect. I am a constant observer. You will see a selection of my own personal photography throughout this book that in some shape or form inspired the work, or vice versa. Sometimes a morning walk on the beach inspires the palette for a room and is drawn out from the many textures and patterns of the earth, and sometimes the work is so much in my head that a sunset reminds me of a completed room. I love the duality of this. It makes for some interesting introspection and reflection. I also just love pretty sunsets and the memory of them. They can live and be just that too a quiet respite after a long day. I am often frustrated when I can't capture what is in front of me, but quickly realize that its true value is in the presence of that exact moment and the mark it will leave on my brain, hopefully to come back later as an inspired palette or just as a great memory.

Since the last book, my husband and I have been fortunate enough to purchase a beach house on the Oregon Coast, one of my favorite places on earth and one of the featured projects in this book as well. This escape from the city has offered countless hours of wandering, endless quiet walks, beautiful sunsets, time with friends old and new, and a respect for the space I require to create and be at my best. This is not something I take for granted by any means and knowing that it could all disappear in a day makes me not only enjoy days spent there more but my days in general. To have a home that takes these quiet moments, these introspective seconds, these root-creating experiences into elements you interact with and live with daily is something I realize I want for others.

Even with this peace I feel as though every project comes to me in a time of need. It may be the urge to work in a certain style or with a type of client, or it may be the need to secure that new project to stay afloat as a business. There are still times when I feel myself feeling low, uninspired, or drained with the day-to-day of business. But these moments create space for thoughtful investigation into a new lifestyle, family dynamic, set and setting, and more, and I crave that newness.

I'd also be lying if I didn't say I also crave feeling wanted or chosen for the project. That's just the human condition keeping you honest. Being a creative is weird and complex like that. You are constantly battling with the desire to create in a bubble and have that work be accepted without change or adjustment, like the painter or photographer who creates a body of work that will ultimately hang in a gallery for viewing. There is no going back once the work is on the wall; the work

is the work, and the viewer will either respond and connect, or not.

But that is not really how interior design works. There are multiple stakeholders at the table, from the client to the designer, and everyone needs to feel heard in order to reach a successful result. The client can foresee several different outcomes for a space before ever interviewing you for a job, and those all need to be considered and dissected to understand what is the most honest version of their space. The designer can also interpret the space in many different ways, usually taking cues from four different points of view before a look and feel is chosen. To fully appreciate the designer's perspective, I'd like to break down these four points.

The client. This includes their history, wants, needs, definitions of comfort, etc. The client will come to their project with preconceived thoughts of what the outcome is going to be. Maybe this is a forever home they have dreamed of for many years, or maybe this is the start of a new chapter in their life when they are downsizing and daring to imagine a different life from how they have lived before. It is my job to extrapolate all of this from them in one way or another, and that job can sometimes be difficult. People can be shy, and trust is earned when we share our innermost desires about how a space can serve us best. Getting to the root of what people want, what comfort means to them, how this space will function for their life and not the life we think they lead, and so on and so forth is the true work. The design beyond that is the given. I've learned over my time in this job that the more honest you are with the client, the more honest the client feels they can be with you. The truth will come out eventually, so it's best we explore what true means to them at the start and not find out once they have moved in. Clients have also asked me to suggest what might be true for them. This could be about the simplest detail, like what my favorite bedding is or what I think about a specific piece of art. If a client requests help with these details, it means you have earned the trust, you have built the bridge, and that feeling is incomparable.

The architecture. This includes its role in defining or juxtaposing with the intended style of the interior of the home. This point of view can be a tricky one for some, and honestly there are many ways you can go about this. The architecture of the home, whether existing or to be built, must be referenced in one way or another on the inside of the home. Full stop. How one goes about deciding what to reference is completely up for debate. You could have a classic San Francisco Victorian home reimagined inside and out. The bones of the home may be respectfully honored and brought back to life as they were intended originally, and the interiors taken very contemporary and minimally, reflecting the modern tastes of its current owners. Fine. You could also cover the entire inside in Victorian wallpaper, furniture, and lighting. Also fine. You could bridge the gap as well—and this, I think, is where the magic happens. In the mix of both worlds, old and new, we find the complex and interesting. For example, you could keep the bones, respectful of the past, and honor its initial intent, while inside you could play with contemporary lighting and mix in furniture from different periods that reference both today and yesterday, creating something that is less an exercise in precision and more a story of the current owners and what they value and see when they look at the home. Like I said, this point is a place for much debate, and I honestly don't know if there is a right answer besides that what is right is what comes from honest and thoughtful conversations.

Set and setting. This includes all that informs a space in terms of its climate, function, and surrounding nature. I live in the Pacific Northwest, where most of our projects reside, and there is a specific light quality here that reflects the many colors that make up the natural elements around. I try my best to listen to those cues when designing a space from the inside out. As I said many times in the last book, nature wins. I am in the camp that believes that we should honor the place where we reside and not try to push too much against it as it will make things feel out of place. For example, there are white paint colors that work in Seattle that just don't work in California, and vice versa. It's also important to understand the vernacular of the place where you are. Are you in a city, the beach, the forest? How are you referencing this in the project? And I don't mean to emulate the homes around me with signs that say, "Beach this way," or something similar. I know where the beach is—I am here, we are here. You can smell it; it infects every aspect of living here. Simply put, look outside and let that guide you.

The designer. This includes their history and what they come to the project with. This point of the view is for many reasons the least important, but it is still a point of view that offers guidance. People come to me for many reasons. They may have seen one of my projects in a magazine or picked up the last book, followed me on Instagram, or even Googled "Seattle interior designer." Regardless of how or why someone decides to hire me and start down the road of design, we are part of this process together now.

Knowing how to hire an interior designer is almost as important as trusting the one you end up with. I have found there are three types of designers out there. There is the type who has a very clear vision of their design, and it doesn't change from project to project. Hiring one of these designers is all about wanting that exact look with little to no intervention. Then there is the type of designer who is what I call a "taskmaster." This type of designer isn't here to insert themselves a ton into the overall look of the project; they are purely there to bring the client's dreams to reality, and there is no common thread to the work they complete. The third type of designer is who I identify with. Our work has a thread through it and a point of view you may be able to suss out if you were to stumble upon it, but it is still client and project specific. It doesn't take itself too seriously and understands that a home that meets the functional and comfort needs of that client outweighs any grand aesthetic stroke. The clients who feel they are being heard, respected, and understood has way more value than any ego I may have and are going to be much happier in their home that they feel true ownership over than a home that feels unreal to them.

Before diving into the actual design, these four points of view are how I organize every project's unique look and feel—a collection of imagery that evokes the mood and atmosphere for the project, whether that be images of fine art, nature, textures, finishes, etc. The look and feel becomes a guide for the design decisions ahead and may even go through a few iterations before everyone can see a glimpse of the end result of this process. I also want to leave room for chance and exploration outside the established look and feel, because this creates space for the pieces or strokes that make a space feel collected versus decorated. In the end, the goal is to create a space that feels warm, welcoming, and true.

Before writing, I asked people what they would like to hear from me in this book. A resounding amount wanted to learn more about who I am as a person who happens to do this job. I think we all walk some sort of crooked line each day, a line defined by our life, past, present, and future. My line is no different from anyone else's in that it has challenges that are personal, hopes that are wild, dreams that sometimes aren't met, and joys that are yearned to be cherished and held on to longer.

To be honest, I am not a present person. It could be that to do what I do for work and run a business at the same time requires a lack of presence in the current moment and more foresight into what is next, how it will affect my present, and how my past has brought me here. I also worry a lot. I worry about how I am perceived by my peers, my clients, the internet, and even my close friends and family. But I also have great love for my work, excitement, and a want to do better and be better.

Why am I mentioning this? It all has to do with the creative process. The mind you bring to design is all of things that make you you. Without all these ingredients, good and bad, you don't get the full picture. Everyone is coming to this process with baggage, and we need to unpack it before starting our work. I need the baggage of a client as much as the good stuff to understand them. I need the baggage of a client as much as When disagreements arise or an angry email comes in, I remind myself: to never pretend to understand anyone's journey. That angry email isn't about the subject matter most of the time; it's a product of a bad day, expectations not being met, a loss of control, etc. We all do this. We are products of our past, present, and future. My work, what I put out into the world, is all of this.

To understand more about me as a person with this job, allow me to dig a bit deeper, past the surface. Here goes.

I was a weird kid. I say this with the utmost respect for Little Me. Like many not-yet-out queer creative kids, I wanted to walk my own path in a world that tried to fit me into a mold. I was adopted and grew up in a well-off area of New England, and while I always had my needs met, what I craved was to be understood and valued as a creative. Hiding, secrecy, and shyness permeated most of my life as I felt I could not express

myself freely. I was not popular in school—ever. I was, in fact, ridiculed and left out by others during most of my school years until college. What is the same about me then and now is that I have always enjoyed my alone time more than being with others.

Upon entering college, a place where I met people from different backgrounds, unlike my childhood home, I was accepted a bit more by other; but the damage had been mostly done at this point, and I had little to no trust in people like me or who wanted to be friends with me . I retreated into myself for most of this time as well. I took long walks at night to pass the time, dream of things beyond my mind, wish for acceptance that was, in reality, in front of me. I was, however, also finally able to create and express myself with wild abandon, and create I did. I excelled in school once and was able to focus on my voice for the first time. Looking back at the work I did in college I can't believe how honest it was about my state of mind at the time. I was wrestling with my sexuality while stuck in a place with few friends who could help in that department, and it was clear that the only way I dealt with it was through my work. The secrets could be disguised in a painting or installation. I could hide behind a camera lens and quietly hope that the viewer would hear my cries for help and acceptance. There were shows of mine so personal and exposing that I would rescind invites to my family members who were proud of me. I was too fearful of them seeing the real me when I wasn't ready.

My mental state was not the best during and a bit after college. I graduated, was lost like most, and stumbled for the next few years in and out of jobs that didn't satisfy my need to create. When I finally came out to my friends and family, I felt a momentary sense of relief that I was my true, authentic self. This was short-lived, however, as I quickly realized that my sexuality was just one part of me. Now we are chipping away at an honest depiction of what was to come of me as an adult.

I felt a different kind of alive the first time I saw the Oregon Coast, where I write this today. I was twenty-five at the time, unsure of my next steps, but blown away by beauty and nature that was bigger than anything going on in my life. The place was Cape Kiwanda, about an hour and a half from where I spend half of my time now. It was November and I was visiting friends who lived in Portland. We hiked, we ate, we reconnected after years apart, and I decided right then and there that I needed to be closer to the feelings I had on the coast more frequently. I stumbled through the next few years in Portland and visited the coast a few times with friends and felt the same draw, one that is still in me today. The draw that makes me walk for hours on the beaches or in the forest, trying to feel something, anything. That presence that I am still after.

I wrote about my early days in Seattle in the last book. I had moved there when I was twenty-seven, after two years in Portland, so I won't get into it again here. (If you haven't read At Home, here is my subtle pitch to go buy it.) Now, this is my present. On a weekly basis, I swear I am going to close the firm, end my design practice, and try my hand at several things, from painting to ghost designing to running a coffee shop. My present is pure juxtaposition. Sometimes I live and work in the busy city of Seattle, a city that birthed my design firm, introduced me to so many people, gave me so many opportunities. A city that also doesn't feel like mine anymore. Like many cities, it hurts too. The haves and the have-nots are exposed more so in a city than other places I have found, and the sadness of this affects me a lot. A city can also invigorate and motivate. In the city I can see clients, projects in progress, be with my team and personally with my friends. I get a lot done there, or so it seems. The other half of my life is spent in Cannon Beach, Oregon, at our beach house—a luxury that is afforded ironically by not closing the firm and ending my design practice. To my husband's dismay, this is where I feel truly myself, and I would move here permanently if I could. He likes the back and forth, and because his head is firmly planted in reality, we do not live here full time. I trust him; he's right.

Our house is a block from the shore and each morning I am here, rain or shine, I take my dog George for a forty-five-minute walk on the beach in a giant circle. This is my idea of pure heaven. This is my alone time, where I can shut off or on, depending on the day. I look around and this place looks like it's right out of a Nancy Meyers movie, and I am the leading character. Our property is two little five-hundred- square-foot houses next to each other. Everything was built in 1940 and one of the buildings was once a garage before being turned into what would equate to a studio apartment. During the day, Justin works in one house while I work in the other. My breaks here are more walks to the beach versus watching TV, or something less fulfilling. I can still feel alone and sad and unsure here, but when I do I let the ocean heal me.

My present also involves the work we do, some of which you will view in this book. The work involves a lot of people, time, patience, hardships, mistakes, hurt feelings, new ideas, and big wins for us and the people inhabiting the spaces. I exist in this industry and have been given a platform to express the thoughts that come into my head if I wanted to—and sometimes I do. I don't like that one of the only ways to get visibility in this industry is through wealth, access, and connections. I feel like an absolute hypocrite most of the time as well. I work for the 1 percent of the 1 percent and cater to their needs, and I am in turn part of that 1 percent. I am not for one moment going to complain about any of this, but context is very important and understanding your circumstances and opportunities allows space for thought and intention. Our clients' means allow us to create interesting and complicated homes that without those means would be quite challenging—not impossible, but very difficult.

I have talked about the past; I have talked about the present; the future is hard for me. I have always been the type of person to keep my head down and focus on what is in front of me regarding work and stay as present as possible in that. I am an interior designer right now, but I am a creative first and foremost and I'll be the first one to admit that maybe this will morph into some other creative outlet, or maybe I will continue to hone this craft which I love so much and has given me so much satisfaction all these years. My point is that no matter the path, take it. Don't be afraid to fail, because failures are just lessons you have yet to learn.

FAMILY COMFORT

Just east of Seattle hides a small neighborhood featuring some incredible waterfront homes with views to the west. My clients, with whom I am close and have worked on three other homes, decided to escape the city, as their family was growing. Their traditional home in the city, at times, felt difficult to modernize and make their own. They loved its traditional bones but often felt that if they intervened too much, the home would lose its character. They found a great lot in this neighborhood, with a spec home being built that fit their needs functionally but not all their wants aesthetically. This type of project has become more common for me recently: stepping in halfway through construction of a spec home and joining forces with the developer to align the finishes with the clients' wants to create a home that is truly theirs.

This new home spoke to their need for more space, and, while traditional in nature, it had the potential for a lighter feel with contemporary elements. Although this home is not on the beach,

I wanted to mimic the colors and textures that emerge when sky meets water. The primary bedroom is reminiscent of the start of a summer sunset, with its warm tones and blue hues that almost disappear. The dining room has one of my favorite shades of green, picked up from the rug. The family room is a mixture of barely-there blues, greens, and naturals, with a saturation of golden wheat in the rug, evoking colors that appear just as the sun sets.

Texture is paramount in the quest for comfort and for breaking up endless walls of white paint. Grass cloth is a material I often use to change the entire feel of a room, so, in this house, I used five different grass cloths along with seven wallpapers, allowing them to set a separate but continuous mood.

I have had dreams of the next chapters with these clients and the homes we will work on together. I'll be reaching toward comfort and warmth first but always want to push the envelope a bit more each time.

THROUGH A SIMILAR LENS

Our reimagination of this Ralph Anderson house started with clients who had lusted over the property for many years before it finally became available, right as the last of their kids were leaving the nest and the couple were transitioning their lives. The house's tree surroundings informed all our decisions.

This was a collector's home, an entertainer's home, not a cozy family home, which our clients desired The middle floor, which holds the kitchen, dining, and living rooms, is one long space with little to no division, and designing it was one of the biggest challenges I have faced in my career. The bedroom, on the third floor, is long and narrow with a support beam in the middle of the room, and it is flanked on two sides by French doors, allowing in amazing light that is filtered through trees.

I opted to keep all the walls a warm white and draw the attention to the door trims, grass shades, and exterior. The furnishings are clean and contemporary yet textured and layered. Of note is the dining table, the base of which was made from the material of a much smaller dining table the wife's father had made many years prior that no longer suited the needs of the clients. We kept the design of the legs, used the original top for bracing, and had a travertine top made. Old meets new, and the memories continue.

These client meetings are some of my favorite memories of my career. We felt an instant connection and related in our love for photographing the darkness and solitude of mysterious nature that makes up the Pacific Northwest. That energy and color story, the architecture, and the clients' calm and supportive nature all are the building blocks of this project, and I will remember our time together forever.

ALL SMILES

This project was my first after the initial silence following the shutdown in March 2020. The family that lived on the property in the original 1,100-square-foot home loved the neighborhood and wanted to stay but needed to build a larger home for their growing household. My team and I were hired right at the start of the project along with the architect to holistically create a language and program for the home. This was the clients' first time doing anything like this and they entered this two-year project with grace, trust, and more smiles than I can imagine ever having while building a house from the ground up during a worldwide pandemic.

The interiors are layered in classic and contemporary styles, but most importantly they are thoughtful to the way the clients wanted to live. Of much debate in the design industry is the white kitchen, and I get it. White can come off as boring. We kept the color traditional but opted for a beautiful hand-poured tile that leaned more greige and took it to the ceiling on the three walls of the space. We also warmed the white of the cabinets, used unlacquered brass plumbing and lights, and added an oak island with vertical V-groove detailing to break up the design. The custom walnut dining table will be there for the family for decades to come, and we paired that with contemporary lighting from Lindsey Adelman to allow every decorative piece in that room to sing.

The primary bedroom's palette is based on a few photos I took of the beach in high summer. Bright, textural, and warm and cool at the same time, it offers a few places to just sit and relax before taking on the rest of the day. There is nothing serious about the house and I like that. It's easy, collected, and, like the owners, infectiously happy.

MONTLAKE SHADE

My husband and I almost bought this 1920s Tudor-style house when it came up for sale because I loved its location, scale, and charm; but, in the end, it wasn't quite right for us. It was funny to me, then, that the new owners, a young gay couple around our age, called on me to decorate it. It was a great connection at our first meeting, and off we went.

With the clients' directives to add more color, push them outside their comfort zone, and consult on the start of an art collection, we got to work on the living room, dining room, den, primary bedroom, and media room. The rooms are on the small side in this home, and abundant landscaping around the house limits the amount of light coming through the windows. So, we leaned into it and went as cozy as possible. The palette of the house, for me, is all about the ghost notes within the scheme—for example, the Yves Klein blue of the Bari Ziperstein vases in a room full of quiet earth tones; the gold velvet pillows and the punchy tones of the overscaled painting by Jay Stern in the den. This challenged me, as I often stay conservative and allow the stuff of life to be the ghost notes.

I think the basement media room is my favorite, with its dark blue grass cloth walls, custom matching sectional, and marbled wallpaper on the ceiling as a collaboration from our friends at Zak and Fox and Apparatus. The ceilings are low and there is little to no natural light, which means this room has just one use: pure relaxation. This house may not be my clients' forever home, but it certainly got them off to a great start and unleashed a desire for collecting local and emerging art.

TOM BIANCHI   63 E 9TH STREET

SATURATION AND LIGHTNESS

I love working in California and have almost moved there countless times during periods of transition. I still think about it. Most of my work has been in West Hollywood and the like, which has a completely different vibe from this project in Manhattan Beach. On days I was visiting the project, I loved being able to wake up early and walk the beaches to gather myself before a day of meetings.

The goal for this project was to turn a less-than-successful builder-grade home into something that spoke to the clients. They were inspired by the softer tones of Scandinavian design and wanted to pair that with a nod to the location, while also incorporating comfort and function in a space that is home to two very active children. This project challenged me to take the colors I normally use and add cream to them, so

to speak. One color you see throughout the project was described to me as chalkboard green, but it took some time to nail it down and then translate it from paint to many other materials.

We changed light fixtures, hardware, and mirrors, and painted spaces in colors you might find in an ice cream shop. The light in California is different from the light in Seattle, so we viewed and decided everything on-site to ensure the tones and qualities were right for the vibe of the space.

This home is about good tea, backyard lunches, and countless walks to the beach. My clients and I bonded over flowers (she was a wedding planner and I had just gotten married). And they challenged me to think about color in a different way while still staying true to my vision for the home.

THE NEXT CHAPTER

I love designing a condo, an apartment, any small space in general. It requires thinking outside the box, sticking to your needs, and sourcing the best of the best since the square footage doesn't go on forever.

These clients had lived in Florida before deciding to relocate to Seattle to be close to their two sons. They were aware that their personal style might not jibe with the Pacific Northwest and this contemporary condo they had acquired. The first conversations we had were about how they needed me to show them what true Downtown Seattle living was, or at least my version of it. They also wanted help curating a collection of some local art, which I am always excited to do.

The condo had been previously designed and decorated by Seattle design legend Rocky Rochon, someone I have yet to meet but very much look up to. I wanted to create a new space for these clients, of course, but I would be lying if I said I didn't have Rocky in the back of my mind the whole time. The space is all windows, and during the winter, the gray sky can be a bit cold. You can't ignore it, but you can balance it. We created two living room areas, one a bit more formal than the other, but both complementing and speaking to each other. There isn't a ton of color in this project, at least eye-catching color: it is a palette of the Seattle sky infused with golden and rusted hues to balance all the cool tones.

The primary bedroom, with its silk walls and wool carpet, might be my favorite bedroom we have ever done; it is the definition of cozy and collected. This project also shows how I build rooms on the texture scale, similarly to how a designer might design a room with solids and prints in small, medium, and large scale.

These spaces grab attention with their comfort level, successful lighting, and interesting juxtaposition first, and then in experiencing the rooms, the textures reveal themselves one by one. Like a song, no one instrument plays louder than the next.

EILEEN GRAY

Joel Meyerowitz — Provincetown

STUDIO KO

WASHINGTON COAST MOOD

I have been coming to Pacific Beach and Seabrook for almost ten years now. My first experience there was doing a show house with *Sunset Magazine* and falling in love with the Pacific Northwest in a way I hadn't yet experienced. I like quiet, I like solitude, but I also like the option to engage as well when I feel a bit cooped up, and this town has that in spades.

This home was a ground-up that was to be a vacation home for a family who lived just south of Seattle. They planned on entering it into the rental program as well, but that was not the outcome. About halfway through the process and through the pandemic, they decided this home would become their primary residence, so we shifted some designs to adapt to their new plans. The directive was a non-themey house on the beach that was comfortable above all else.

To be honest, my biggest root inspiration for the house and its design goes back to the first night I spent in Seabrook, around 2013. I was there for meetings and had a small house to myself that came with a hot tub. I spent the first night in that hot tub staring at the sky and all the stars, feeling so small and infinite all at once. This, along with a long walk on the vast beachront the following morning, became root experiences for me in my own quest for happiness and a place to rest my overactive brain. Coming back many years later to work on this house brought back all those quiet thoughts immediately. This house is about good coffee, fabrics that you want to rest your head on, beach treasures, and our wild imaginations.

GYMNASIUM LUKE SMALLEY

History of Information Graphics

MADISON PARK WARMTH

These clients, originally from Vermont and Seattle, had lived in San Francisco before moving to Seattle with their two young sons to live closer to the wife's family. They settled into a beautiful area near the water just east of the city. The house, which on the outside was traditional, would lead you to believe that the inside was much different than was the case. In fact, the interior had been updated in a contemporary style by the previous owners, which is what drove the aesthetics of the project for me.

Here is another example of using textured grass cloth in numerous spaces to deal with all the white walls. The house is surrounded by big green trees all year long, so we brought that inside with the green color of the grass cloth. The design is casual yet hardworking—a little bit Seattle and a little bit California relaxed. Aside from the green throughout, I also had a bug in me that wanted to infuse a goldenrod color throughout in different ways—a rug here, a slipcover there, and the tone of oak we juxtaposed against the dark walnut floors. One thing I like to do is make sure none of the furniture legs match the flooring, so the distinct stop and start between them creates interest.

This primary bedroom is favorite of mine. While no one needs a whole seating area in their bedroom, the long scale of this space called for it. It also provides a second office location. I love a primary bedroom seating area for slow mornings when you don't need to rush or for early evenings when you want to enjoy some time away from the activities in the rest of the house.

ROTHKO THE COLOR FIELD PAINTINGS

BASQUIAT FONDATION LOUIS VUITTON Gallimard

BALANCING ACT

We were given carte blanche in designing this home, a 1920s Spanish Colonial in the exclusive neighborhood of Broadmoor in Seattle. The home was true to the type of homes found in warmer and, quite frankly, more appropriate climates. My initial thought was, how do I make this style fit into the Pacific Northwest but also be true to the house as it exists?

We embarked on an extensive remodel and took away a lot of the frosting added during a previous remodel. The goal was to make the design cleaner, a bit more contemporary in styling, but also true to the architecture. The whites became cooler and less yellow. The floors stayed dark, but as wider planks. The tile and stone were laid to be still interesting and textural, but devoid of period-specific patterns. The lighting became almost exclusively contemporary, and the furnishings mixed mid-century, contemporary, and traditional styles with pieces that would look right at home in a relaxed Santa Barbara estate. The palette for the most part stayed neutral but heavily textured, save for a few splashes of green to relate to the exterior and the Pacific Northwest in general.

This was a large and very rewarding project for me, to be given the clients' trust to think outside of the box and deliver a full vision. Of course, I don't expect every client to come and say, "Go for it!" That would be asking a lot and frankly not my ideal, since I like a lot of client engagement. But this house was not like anything I had ever worked with before, so not only did I learn to recalibrate my thinking and research a new style, but I also discovered what a Spanish Colonial home meant through my eyes, knowing I had my clients' trust for a beautiful home designed for them.

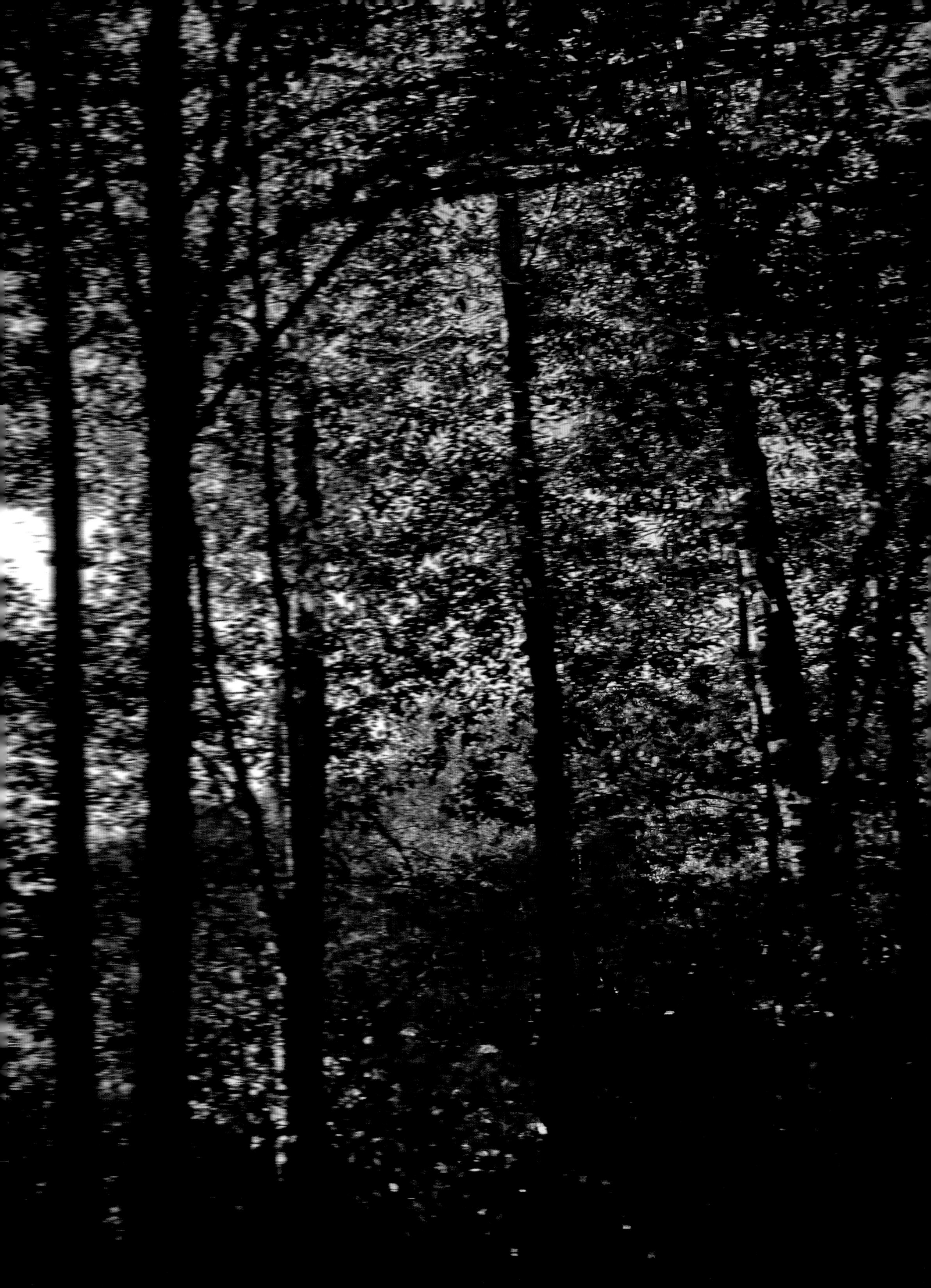

A PIED-À-TERRE

This 1920s bungalow, all but four hundred square feet, is my clients' pied-à-terre in Seattle. I had worked with them on their main residence in Idaho a few years back. We made this small-sized project all about story and having fun, focusing on the cute bungalow aspect of it.

The space consists of a living room, kitchen, small bathroom, and bedroom, each room with its own charm. The bedroom, for example, holds a king-sized bed and essentially nothing else, aside from the built-in cupboards we designed to take the place of the previous standard closet. Thinking like shipbuilders, we included storage wherever we could and thought about multiuse spaces. The palette of greens, pinks, burgundies, dirty beiges, and yellows came from the story that this cottage would give nods to traditional British design. The Marthe Armitage wallpaper in the kitchen was, in fact, printed in the UK. We wanted fabrics that felt collected instead of curated, and a bit "off," like the bedroom's headboard fabric, which was just that right bit of off and unexpected.

The experience of this project taught me to collect what you like without forcing things into context or matching; all will work together as fine pieces and feel uniquely yours, more organic, and less intentionally decorated.

I have some of the best phone calls with these clients, laughing for hours and throwing many ideas back and forth on whatever we are working on. One of them constantly challenges me and then ends every call saying, "I love you, and you are doing great things."

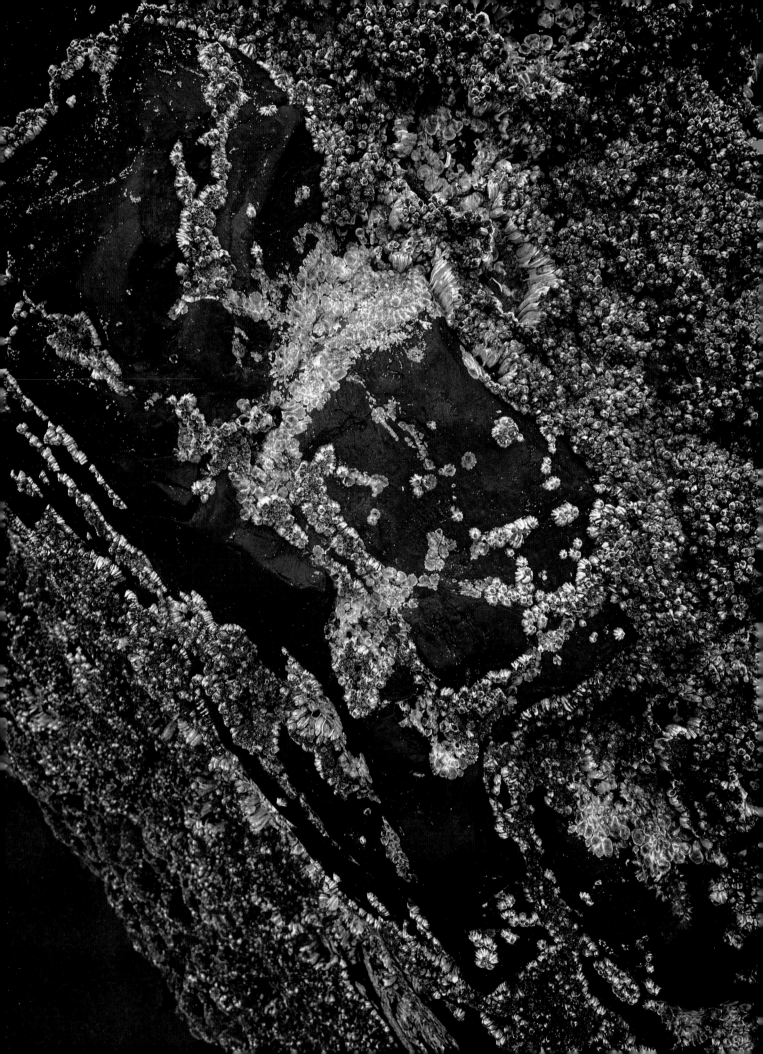

OUR BEACH DREAM

The houses designers do for themselves are often very different from their client work—as they should be. My husband and I bring our own histories to each home we live in, and together we create what is truly ours. Our house in Cannon Beach on the Oregon Coast is vital to our lives just now. It is also a collection of the memories we have with everyone with whom we have shared our home: meals cooked with friends, long walks on the beach with our dogs, important conversations over coffee in the early morning, and laughs from the depths of our bellies on the front lawn.

For me, this house and all it offers is about balance and mindfulness. At a time when I felt lost, distracted, uninspired, and unsure of my path forward, it held me and lifted me up.

A block away from the beach, a long walk with one's thoughts is an easy break from the workday. I have spent countless hours watching the colors shift, feeling the wind blow through me while contemplating my next move. Technically speaking, the 1940 house is two separate structures, essentially, two studio apartments, with the main kitchen inside one of the homes. While here, just the two of us, we spend our workdays in separate places doing our own thing. At night, dinner is prepared in the main house, usually followed by a nightcap in the form of a walk to view the sunset. We slow down here; we revitalize here; we are in tune with what matters most to us. Here I have come to know myself deeper. I am aware of what is needed for me to thrive and create in a way that prioritizes space and care and intention. This house is not a given, and the greatest lesson I have learned through having it is that I need to find those things in my daily life regardless of location.

FINAL THOUGHTS

One of the biggest takeaways over the past couple years of being an interior designer, creative, whatever you want to call it, is there is no one way to feed the machine that is our mind. Some require assignments to thrive; some require complete creative freedom to release the truest form of their art. Some need space; some need constant collaboration. Some need hours-long walks to clear their brain and only delve into the work when the spirit calls them, so to speak. There is no right way. It's a constant evolution where you hopefully gain a better understanding of your needs as a "painter" in this world. I have learned to not judge what shape the canvas takes. All of it—whether a sketch, a room, a photograph, a walk—is part of the journey of getting out into the world what is in your head.

Might I suggest a long walk?

ACKNOWLEDGMENTS

This book is for the dreamers, the wanderers, the mindful and for those still searching. Let the world envelop you with its light and have the grace to accept it.

This book is also for my husband whose patience and way of looking at the world brings me peace. Your love and support are more than I could ever hope for.

To my friends and colleagues, you inspire, challenge, and lift me up.

To my clients, thank you for letting me into your life and allowing me to create homes that hopefully make your life easier and show you a new kind of beauty. You bring life beyond a dream to me.

And to you, dear reader, this book is a result of the success of the first and your belief in me. Thank you.

THE AUTHOR

Brian lives in Seattle, Washington, with his husband, Justin, and their two dogs, George + Oliver.

SOURCES

ARTISTS & GALLERIES

Victoria Morris
www.victoriamorris.com

Bari Zipperstein
www.barizipperstein.com

Kippi Leonard
www.kipleeart.com

Seattle Art Source
Seattle, WA
www.seattleartsource.com

Lydia Bassis
lydiabassis.com

Mirena Kim
www.Mirenakim.com

FURNITURE

This is Urban Made
Seattle, WA
www.thisisurbanmade.com

Design Within Reach
www.dwr.com

Inform Interiors
Seattle, WA
www.informinteriors.design

Casssina
www.cassina.com

Egg Collective
New York, NY
www.eggcollective.com

Lawson Fenning
Los Angeles, CA
www.lawsonfenning.com

RT Facts
Kent, CT
www.rtfacts.com

Stahl + Band
Venice, CA
www.stahlandband.com

Nickey Kehoe
Los Angeles, CA
www.nicekykehoe.com

O&G Collective
Warren, RI
www.oandgstudio.com

Pinch
London, England
www.pinchdesign.com

Hollywood at Home
Los Angeles, CA
www.hollywoodathome.com

Made Goods
www.madegoods.com

Gubi
www.gubi.com

Martin & Brocket
Los Angeles, CA
www.martinandbrockett.com

Josh Green Design
www.joshgreendesign.com

Summer Studio
www.summerstudiodesign.com

Disc Interiors
www.discinteriors.com

Kalon Studios
www.kalonstudios.com

De La Espada
www.delaespada.com

LIGHTING

Vaughan Designs
New York, NY and other locations
www.vaughandesigns.com

Lindsey Adelman
Los Angeles, CA / New York, NY
www.lindseyadelman.com

Pletz
New York, NY
www.pletzmade.com

Danny Kaplan
New York, NY
www.dannykaplanstudio.com

Visual Comfort
www.visualcomfort.com

Allied Maker
www.alliedmaker.com

Apparatus
Los Angeles, CA / New York, NY
www.apparatusstudio.com

Workstead
New York, NY
www.workstead.com

Stone and Sawyer
www.stoneandsawyer.com

Made by Hand
www.madebyhand.dk

Cuff Studio
www.cuffstudio.com

The Urban Electric Company
www.urbanelectric.com

Lostine
www.lostine.com

SHOPS & SHOWROOM

Garde Shop
Los Angeles, CA
wwwgardeshop.com

Kelly Forslund
Seattle, WA
www.kellyforslund.com

Erik Waldorf
Seattle, WA
www.erikwaldorf.com

Barbara Otto
www.barbaraotto.com

Jennifer West
Seattle, WA
www.jwshowroom.com

Trammell Gagne
Seattle, WA
www.tgshowroom.com

Agency Etoile
www.agencyetoile.com

Dixon Group
Seattle, WA
www.thedixongroup.net

Seattle Lighting
Seattle, WA
www.seattlelighting.com

Chown Hardware
www.chown.com

Perrenials and Sutherland
www.perennialsandsutherland.com

Housewright
Seattle, WA
www.Hosuewright.com

TEXTILES

Zak + Fox
www.zakandfox.com

Glant
www.glant.com

Rogers & Goffigon
www.rogersandgoffigon.com

Kerry Joyce
www.kerryjoyce.com

Clarence House
www.Clarencehouse.com

Romo
www.romo.com

Larsen Fabrics
www.larsenfabrics.com

Moore & Giles
www.mooreandgiles.com

Phillip Jefferies
www.phillipjefferies.com

Armadillo
www.armadillo-co.com

Zoffany
www.zoffany.sandersondesigngroup.com

Kufri
www.kufrilifefabrics.com

Stark
www.starkcarpet.com

Kush
Portland, OR
www.kushrugs.com

Mclaurin & Piercy
www.mclaurinandpiercy.com

Perennials Fabrics
www.perennialsfarbics.com

Samuel & Sons
www.samuelandsons.com

Rose Tarlow
www.rosetarlow.com

Thibaut
www.thibautdesign.com

Pindler
www.pindler.com

Castel
www.castelmaison.com

Studio Four NYC
www.studiofournyc.com

Brentano
www.brentanofabrics.com

First Edition
28 27 26 25 24   5 4 3 2 1

Text © 2024 Brian Paquette
Photographic credits:
© 2024 Harris Kenjar 22, 24-5, 27-32, 34, 38-41, 43-7, 51-3, 56, 58-61,
   64-73, 76, 78-80, 82, 84-5, 87, 90, 93-6, 99-102, 104-06, 108-15,
   117, 120-5, 127-9, 132-3, 136-8, 140-8, 150-1
© 2024 Miranda Estes 8-9, 15, 18, 154-60, 162-69, 171-81, 183-8,
   190-5, 198-9, 201-9, 212-17, 220-2, 224-38,
© 2024 Brian Paquette 2, 6, 10, 19, 20, 23, 26, 33, 35, 36, 42, 48-9, 50,
   54, 57, 62-3, 74, 77, 81, 83, 86, 88, 91, 92, 97, 98, 101, 102, 107, 116,
   118, 126, 130-1, 134, 139, 149, 152, 161, 170, 182, 189, 196, 200, 210-11,
   218, 223, 239, 240, 243
© 2024 Aaron Leitz 4, 242, 244
End pages courtesy ZAK + FOX

Published by
Gibbs Smith
P.O. Box 667
Layton, Utah 84041
1.800.835.4993 orders
www.gibbs-smith.com

Gibbs Smith is an employee-owned, B Corp certified independent
publisher and distributor. We commit to carbon neutrality and reduce
what we can and offset what we are not yet able to. Our physical office
facilities, business travel, production/printing, and outbound shipping
are all carbon neutral.

Designed by Virginia Brimhall Snow
Printed and bound in China
Gibbs Smith books are printed on either recycled, 100% post-consumer
waste, FSC-certified papers or on paper produced from sustainable
PEFC-certified forest/controlled wood source. Learn more at www.
pefc.org.

Library of Congress Control Number: 2023942686
ISBN: 978-1-4236-6510-6

Printed in China using FSC® Certified materials

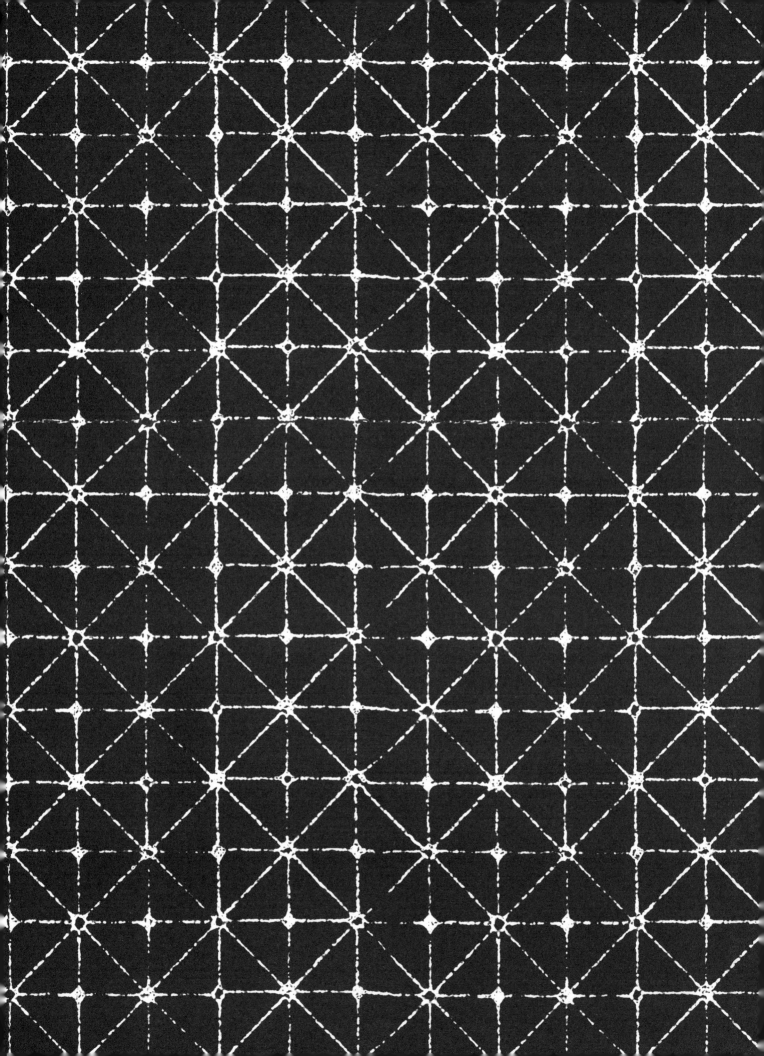

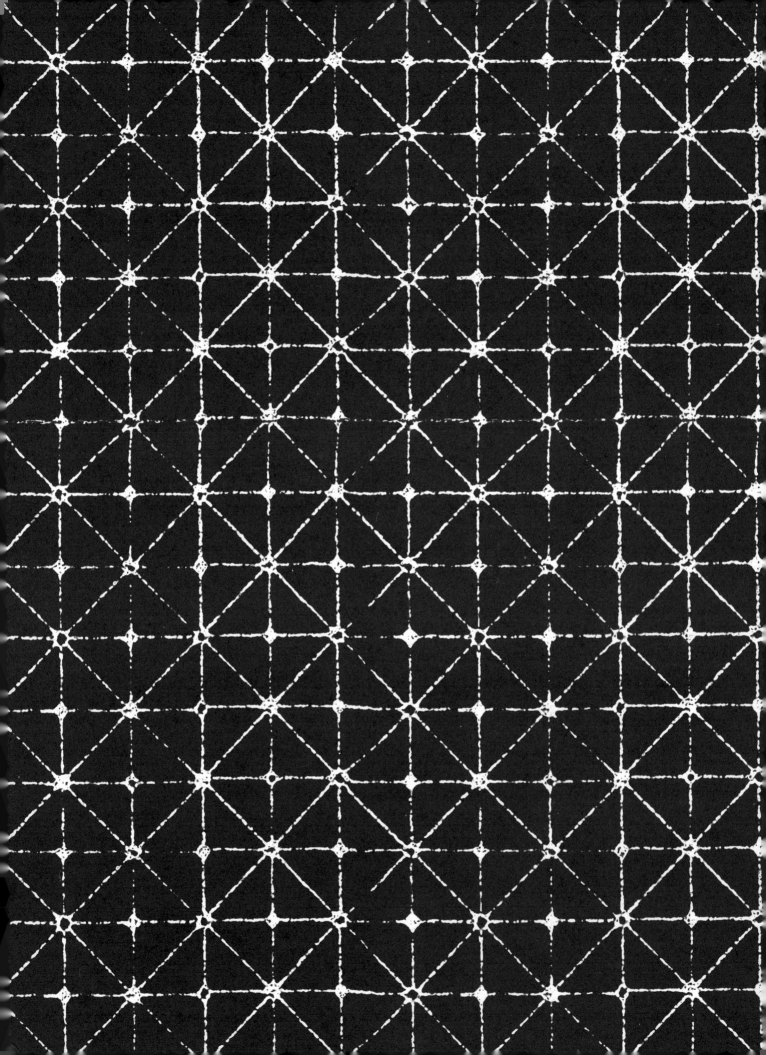